Original title:
The Joy of Thanksgiving Reflections

Copyright © 2024 Creative Arts Management OÜ
All rights reserved.

Author: Thomas Sinclair
ISBN HARDBACK: 978-9916-94-326-7
ISBN PAPERBACK: 978-9916-94-327-4

Autumn Crescendos

Leaves are falling, crunch beneath my feet,
Pumpkin spice and sweets, such a treat.
A turkey dance, oh what a sight,
My cat steals the pie, what a fright!

Family gathers, all in a rush,
Grandma's secret, a recipe crush.
The table set, but where's the wine?
Oops, I drank it all, that's just fine!

Football games, we cheer and we shout,
A cousin trips, falls over the sprout.
Scattered dishes, the dog's on the prowl,
Chasing crumbs, with a happy growl!

As the day ends, laughter fills the air,
One last slice that I'm too full to share.
We'll cherish these moments, what a delight,
Till next year's feast, oh what a night!

The Spirit of Togetherness

Gather 'round, my crazy crew,
With burnt pies and gravy stew.
A turkey dance, oh what a sight,
We're thankful for this silly night.

Uncle Fred dropped the rolls again,
And Aunt Sue's jokes are slightly strange.
We laugh till we can't breathe so well,
As we sip on juice from the wishing well.

Gathering Around the Table

Dinner's served, but where's the chair?
Uncle Joe's hogging all the air.
Passed potatoes, a flying feat,
One more helping? Oh, can't be beat!

Mismatched socks and stories tall,
Who knew family could be this small?
We clash with laughter, not with fear,
And toast to all that brings us here.

Triumph of Togetherness

In the kitchen, chaos reigns,
Spilled cider on the window panes.
But oh, the joy of tasty bites,
Even if grandma's food ignites!

The dog is eyeing all the fries,
As cousins play their little lies.
"Did you really bake this pie?" they ask,
While I just smile and take the task.

Savoring Moments Shared

Laughter echoes, what a mess,
Between the fun and mishaps, bless.
Grandma's myths of days gone by,
All half true, which makes us sigh.

With every bite, a funny tale,
About old socks and the neighbor's hail.
We treasure each ridiculous gaffe,
As we join for a thankful laugh.

Grateful Hearts Unite

Gather 'round the turkey, oh what a sight,
Cousins in pajamas, a comical fright.
Laughter spills over like the gravy so brown,
A feast for the ages, let's all wear a crown.

Auntie's green beans, not quite so refined,
Uncle Joe's jokes, ones that are blind.
With pie on our faces, we dance in delight,
Grateful hearts unite, what a quirky sight!

Nature's Bounty

Pumpkins and apples, a farmhouse delight,
Squash that sings melodies, oh what a night!
The corn on the cob jumps right off the plate,
And squirrels, they plot, while we celebrate fate.

Nature's own buffet, a feast so divine,
While I trip on the pumpkin, I still sip my wine.
Sunshine and brown leaves swirl wildly around,
Nature's bounty is here, in chaos we're found!

Serenity in Sharing

Pass the mashed potatoes, with a wink and a smile,
The bigger the scoop, the longer the trial.
Sister's sweet potatoes, too sweet to behold,
We finish each bite, though our crises unfold.

A cat on the table? Oh no, what a mess!
Sharing our stories, despite the distress.
Amidst all the chaos, a hug can be found,
Serenity dwells where love does abound.

A Tapestry of Thanks

Crafting a meal like it's modern art,
The turkey's so stuffed, it's more like a cart.
Napkins folded neatly, or not at all,
Creating memories, we share, we enthrall.

Uncle's old tales that he tells every year,
Of how he once danced, and drank too much beer.
We weave all these moments, hilariously grand,
A tapestry of laughs, with our quirky band!

A Feast for the Spirit

Turkey on the table, oh what a sight,
Cousin Joe's bad jokes, they just might bite.
Pumpkin pies piled high, who will take two?
Uncle's snoring loud, clashes with our chew.

Gravy spills like laughter, everywhere it flows,
Grandma's secret recipe, nobody knows.
Laughter fills the air, as we all take a stand,
Dancing like the food, nobody quite planned.

Gentle Hues of Autumn

Leaves fall like confetti, colors bold and bright,
Sweaters itch with joy, in this chilly night.
Squirrels stockpile treats, planning for the cold,
While we stuff our faces, just like we were told.

Candles soft and flickering, casting shadows wide,
While we share our stories, with a spark of pride.
Each chuckle echoes gently, through the autumn air,
As we savor leftovers, without a single care.

Memories in the Making

Family gathered round, like a comical show,
Dishes clanging loud, where did the laughter go?
A spilled glass of cider, oh what a mess!
Yet smiles bloom like pumpkins, no need to impress.

Photos taped on walls, moments meant to last,
Each snapshot a giggle, each moment a blast.
Here's to the silly faces, and the wobbly grin,
Connected by the chaos, where love does begin.

Harvesting Warmth

Hot cocoa in hand, as we warm our feet,
While sharing silly tales, quite the comedic feat.
The dog steals the turkey, oh what a sight,
A chase through the kitchen, what a wild night!

Gratitude flows like cider, sweet and divine,
Between bites of cranberry, and that last glass of wine.
So here's to the laughter, the mess, and the cheer,
With family around, there's nothing to fear!

Bridges of Friendship

Across the table, laughter sings,
As Auntie taps her holy wings.
The turkey wobbles, slightly shy,
While Uncle Fred just starts to cry.

With every toast, we cheer and chime,
Counting blessings, one at a time.
Spilled gravy on his brand-new shirt,
Laughter ensues; oh, how it hurt!

Then comes the pie, a sugary sight,
But Grandma claims it's not quite right.
Her secret spices, a mystery quest,
Leaves us guessing, oh, what a jest!

Through bites and quirks, we find our beat,
In silly tales and tasty treats.
Together we dance, in joy we bask,
Friendship's bridge is all we ask!

Abundance Underfoot

Stuffed chairs and laughter fill the room,
While distant cousins try to zoom.
Pie crumbs scatter, like confetti bright,
As Grandpa naps—what a silly sight!

The table groans under the feast,
With plates piled high, we're not the least.
More stuffing? Oh, don't be absurd!
The buttons on my pants have concurred!

A feast so grand, a carnival flair,
Hiding greens under a pile of care.
We laugh at broccoli, meek and tamed,
In this bonanza, none are ashamed!

But as the meals draw to a close,
We realize, who would've chose?
To eat so much and feel this bliss,
And clearly, there's a crumb out of this!

Crumbs of Contentment

With crumbs of pie on every face,
Each child operates at a fun pace.
A dog sneaks in, a master thief,
Uncle's quick shout brings don't be brief!

Through giggles and playful shoves,
We're reminded of our shared loves.
The little ones argue over a toy,
While Dad scoffs, 'That was pure joy!'

From chatter loud, to moments still,
Finding solace in the thrill.
Crumbs of contentment trail behind,
In every chuckle, happiness we find.

So let us raise a glass and cheer,
To family tales that bring us near.
With each slice shared, we understand,
Life's banquet laid by a caring hand!

Fables of Family

Gather 'round, let's spin some tales,
Of family quirks and candy trails.
An epic clash of jests and fights,
Who knew Aunt Sue could take such bites?

Our traditions twist like turkeys fried,
With dodging skills that can't be denied.
Like Grandma's stuffing, that fought and fled,
It landed smack on Uncle Ted's head!

Fabled moments we cherish oh-so dear,
Debating sports with far too much beer.
Through laughter and love, we ignite the night,
Family tales bring pure delight!

So here's to us, the merry bunch,
As we feast away—let's make it a crunch!
For in every nibble, a story's spun,
And this gathering, oh, it's just begun!

Candles Flicker

Candles flicker, oh what a scene,
Pumpkin pie dreams and whipped cream.
A turkey that's larger than my whole head,
Gravy rivers flowing, enough to be fed.

A table with dishes stacked high to the sky,
A cousin who claims he can bake but won't try.
Laughter erupts with each silly joke,
As Aunt Edna's wig nearly went up in smoke.

Spirits Soar

Spirits soar when dessert is near,
Uncle Joe's dance moves, bless his career!
The wine flows freely like a mischievous sprite,
We toast to the cheese that's not quite right.

A feast fits for kings, yet dogs eye the spread,
While the cat steals the turkey, quite bold and well-fed.
Grandma shows off her floral-print dress,
We snicker and giggle, it's a hilarious mess.

Threads of Gratitude Woven

Threads of gratitude woven with care,
Handmade poppers, what a wild affair!
Grandpa's tall tales stretch longer than the night,
While the kids spin circles on pure delight.

A toast to the bird that was lost in a bet,
The gravy boat tips, oh what a fret!
Yet love wraps around like an old, cozy quilt,
In this circus of family, we laugh until we wilt.

Autumn's Embrace of Thanks

Autumn's embrace, leaves crunch underfoot,
Uncle Bob's deep-fried turkey, not too astute.
We gather around and reminisce the past,
While Dad's good jokes are still unsurpassed.

A table spread wide, with foods to explore,
Cranberries bounce, and someone drops more.
With laughter like echoes that dance through the hall,
This feast is absurd, yet we enjoy it all!

Heartfelt Whispers of Gratitude

Heartfelt whispers, secrets they spill,
Aunt Sue's secret stuffing could give you a thrill.
The kids are plotting to poison the pie,
While Grandpa nods off with a soft, sleepy sigh.

Laughter like bubbles in a fizzy whirlpool,
As cousin Tim trips, a clumsy old fool.
Yet amidst all the chaos, we find what we need,
Gratitude wrapped in laughter's sweet seed.

Bounty of Belonging

Gather round the table wide,
A turkey dance, we can't abide.
Mashed potatoes start to fly,
Who knew they could reach the sky?

Uncle Bob steals all the rolls,
While Aunt Sue hogs the carrot bowls.
Laughter echoes off the walls,
As someone trips and kindly sprawls.

Gravy rivers flood the plates,
With pie that's laced with hilarious fates.
A toast with cider, bubbly bright,
May your pants fit after tonight!

So let us feast and sing our praise,
In this chaotic, loving haze.
With family near and friends so dear,
Thankfulness arrives with all the cheer!

Reflections in a Pumpkin Patch

In a pumpkin patch, we sit and grin,
With faces painted like scared raccoons.
The pies are rolling, oh what a sin,
I swear I saw one hiding at noon.

The grandkids sneak bites of the treat,
While Grandma's still searching for her shoe.
Laughter's the language that we all greet,
With a splash of whipped cream in the queue.

A scarecrow attempts to join the fun,
But stumbles as we all try to chase.
Who knew patching pumpkins could be this run?
It's a harvest of giggles that we embrace.

So as we ponder the autumn sway,
Remember the laughter that brightened our day.
With each silly moment, we gather near,
The pumpkin patch surprises, and we all cheer!

A Tapestry of Thankfulness

In a kitchen filled with fragrant spice,
A mishap! The turkey's way too nice.
Stuffing's dancing, what a sight,
As Grandma's yelling, "Don't turn off the light!"

Sister's burning the cranberry sauce,
While Dad's trying to find a line to toss.
Mom's eyeing the pie with careful ease,
And the dog's underfoot—just hoping to please.

A tapestry of laughter we weave,
As cousins compete to see who can leave.
Tales of old, both sweet and wild,
Make us chuckle like a carefree child.

As we gather the spoons to clean the mess,
We're reminded of moments that we truly bless.
Each bite seasoned with love and delight,
In our quirky, chaotic family night!

The Warmth of Kindred Spirits

Gathered 'round in our crazy best,
Fighting for space, it's a comfy nest.
Aunt and Uncle share their delight,
In stories of mishaps, both silly and bright.

The hot dish tips, we gasp in shock,
But in this crowd, there's always a clock.
Timing's key when pies are near,
A battle unfolds, but we emerge in cheer.

With toasts that make little sense at all,
And kids throwing rolls as we have a ball.
The warmth around us is never far,
Like a cozy quilt or a shining star.

So here's to family, ridiculous and true,
In their laughter, we find glue.
Every bite shared, every joke a delight,
In this gathering, everything feels right!

Blessings Counted in Cornbread

In the kitchen, all the flavors clash,
The cornbread's rising, oh what a splash!
A dash of sugar, just for the fun,
Will it taste good, or just weigh a ton?

Grandma's stuffing, what a wild scene,
She swears it's healthy, oh what a meme!
With each bite, we'd all give a grin,
Hoping that gravy will drown the sin.

Football's on, but we're stuck at the table,
Listening to Uncle Joe tell tales of a fable.
He once caught a fish, or so he claims,
But memory fades when what matters is games.

At the end of the feast, we all sit back,
Counting our blessings, there's not one we lack.
With laughter and love, we share this cheer,
Next year's cornbread, we hope it won't veer!

Nature's Palette of Appreciation

Leaves are falling in a confetti swirl,
Nature's colors, watch them twirl!
Pumpkin pie spice hangs in the air,
Who needs a gym when we've this feast to share?

Squirrels plotting their quiet heist,
Nabbing leftovers, isn't that nice?
A dog on the porch, eyeing the plate,
His droopy face says he just can't wait.

Birds chirping loud, they seem to agree,
We're all thankful, even the bee!
Sharing this picnic, wild and bright,
Oh, nature's laughter is quite the delight!

As we gather 'round, here's what we learned,\nAppreciation's served with a side of concern.
Next year we'll plant, and with care, we'll grow,
More pies, more friends, and laughter in tow!

Harmony in the Gathering

Family's laughter dances in the air,
We're seated together, each with a chair.
A toast to the chaos, it's surely a blast,
Reminiscing on mishaps, oh how they last!

Mom's in the kitchen, a whirlwind of zest,
Stirring the pot like a true culinary quest.
Dad's telling stories of his glory days,
But we're still laughing at his mullet phase.

Cousins are choking on grandma's sweet rolls,
As we navigate gathers and shared family goals.
Did someone bring pie? Or did it get lost?
We'll just take a few bites, whatever the cost!

As the plates clear, we smile and we sigh,
Thankful together, just you and I.
The harmony sings, as joy takes the lead,
We'll savor this gathering, fulfilling the need!

Echoes of Gratitude in the Air

Echoes of laughter ring through the home,
As we gather 'round, there's nowhere to roam.
A toast with some cider, a sip and a cheer,
For everyone's quirks, that's what brings us near.

The kids are running with their turkey hats,
Chasing each other like playful spats.
A splash of cranberry right on my shoe,
Oh, the grace of the party — is that really you?

As stories unwind like a ball of yarn,
We cringingly remember the brotherly scorn.
But hark! The pie calls, we can't let it wait,
That pumpkin perfection is worth the debate.

In the heart of the chaos, we find a calm thought,
With laughter and love, this is what we've sought.
So raise up your glass, let the echoes ring clear,
For gratitude shines through the laughter and cheer!

Threads of Tradition

Grandma's gravy, a science fair,
Floating lumps that dance with flair.
A turkey strutted, bold and proud,
But served with laughter, we're loud and loud.

Uncle Joe drops his plate with flair,
Colliding with Aunt Bea's flowing hair.
Pumpkin pie with a dab of cream,
Three spoonfuls in—it's the ultimate dream.

Football plays in the back of the room,
While kids invade the pantry's gloom.
A feast of chaos, a feast of fun,
All gather 'round, let the games be won.

Mom hurries with a "Please, take a seat,"
As the dog plots his next sly feat.
Each year we gather, the same old crew,
With stories we'll share, and all of it's true.

Embers of Remembrance

A toast to the chef, here's a giggle,
Last year's roast was a real tight wiggle.
Cranberry sauce in a can so round,
Plopped on the plate with a sassy sound.

Old photos show Dad with his beard,
Wonder how much Aunt Sue would've cheered.
Burnt rolls and a flame-fetched roast,
Laughing 'til we're just a silly ghost.

Lively tales, some tall and wild,
Each year they add a brand new child.
Pulling memories from the oven's warmth,
While wild turkey makes a stompin' swarm.

Each bite we take is a treasure chest,
Full of love and a hunger quest.
As laughs echoed from the start to end,
We savor each moment, with family as friends.

Laughter Around the Table

Gather 'round, with glasses in hand,
Uncle Bob knows the awkward stand.
Knock-knock jokes meet stuffing surprise,
As cousins giggle and roll their eyes.

Aunt Pat's fruitcake, a legendary fear,
Echoes of screams when it comes near.
Dad tells the tale of his worst fall,
While the kids all cluster, less than small.

"Last year's turkey had a weird look,"
Laughter bubbles like a well-loved book.
A burned pie that once flared bright,
Now sits as evidence of our plight.

At the heart of it, we gather near,
With goofy jokes and mugs of cheer.
Between the bites, love fills the air,
Around this table, nothing compares.

Cornucopia of Memories

A cornucopia spills, what a sight,
The veggies rolled off, oh what a fright!
Grandpa's tales of the good old days,
Are served with a side of turkey craze.

Cousins start a food throwing war,
A swift green bean right at the door.
Laughter echoes like a sturdy drum,
As we blame the dog for being dumb.

Sweet potatoes wear a crafty glaze,
While Aunt Linda hides her flustered gaze.
"Oh, the pie needs a touch of care!"
Only for it to vanish in thin air.

We toast to mishaps and friendships near,
While sharing secrets loud and clear.
In each hearty laugh and heartfelt tune,
Our family shines like the harvest moon.

Leaves of Thanks

As the leaves crunch underfoot,
I trip and fall, what a hoot!
Grateful for fewer branches,
Laughter bounces, no second chances.

Mashed potatoes in a bowl,
Someone just dropped it, oh what a goal!
Gravy splattered, a festive art,
Sharing giggles warms the heart.

Pumpkin pie with whipped cream swirl,
I sneak a slice, watch my twirl.
Surprise, it's stuck upon my nose,
Thankful for all the silly woes.

A turkey dance, we all take part,
With silly hats and merry hearts.
Thanks for laughter and all the glee,
Join the fun, come laugh with me!

Remembrance in Every Flavor

A feast laid out, a smorgasbord,
Grandma's recipes, a thanking hoard.
She steals a glance, I grab too much,
Dinner's timing, oh, such a clutch!

Cranberries glisten, a platter's pride,
One too many, I take the ride.
They bounce off plates, a sight to see,
Who knew this was such a jubilee?

Uncle Joe talks, detailing pies,
While I'm plotting my next surprise.
"Don't eat too fast!" they all chime in,
But here I go, ready to begin!

The laughter fills the air with cheer,
Each funny story, brings us near.
With every bite and every spill,
Thankful hearts are full, what a thrill!

A Symphony of Smiles

Chairs all squeak as we take our seats,
Sharing jokes and tasty treats.
A trombone made of mashed sweet spuds,
Who knew our table would play like thuds?

A turkey's leg goes flying high,
Like a comet in the pie-filled sky.
Laughter echoes, filling the night,
Here, silly moments feel just right.

The cranberry sauce is a sticky foe,
It slid right off, oh, what a show!
With every fumble and every glance,
Thankful hearts invite a dance.

And as dessert is rolling near,
We sing out loud, we have no fear.
Double helpings of smiles unfold,
This merry feast is pure, pure gold!

Thankful Trails

Down the aisle, we make our way,
Dodging spills in a clumsy display.
A pie falls down, what a big mess,
Still, we laugh and feel so blessed.

Grandpa is snoring, what a sight,
Dreaming of turkey, oh what a bite!
"Don't wake him up," we hold our breath,
Captured in laughter, we dance with death.

The dog sneaks in, a silent thief,
Stealing crumbs, beyond belief.
Thankful for mishaps, none walk away,
Without a chuckle to end the day.

As we gather 'round to say our thanks,
We share our stories, fill the pranks.
In each chuckle and every cheer,
We're thankful for laughter, year after year!

Gratitude's Harvest

Turkey tried to run away,
But ended up as buffet prey.
Pumpkin pie, oh what a sight,
Leftovers in the fridge, what a fright!

Family fights for the last slice,
Though we all know it's not so nice.
Uncle Joe tells the same old joke,
While cousin Tim tries not to choke!

Ha! Who spilled the cranberry sauce?
The dog thinks it's a tasty gloss.
We chuckle at the oddest sights,
While feasting on the epic bites!

Grateful for every crazy face,
These silly moments we embrace.
With laughter echoing through the room,
Abundance flourishes, dispelling gloom!

A Cornucopia of Memories

Gather 'round, it's that time again,
A feast that's awkward for most men.
A cornucopia of delicious treats,
And Grandma's dance that can't be beat!

Pies stacked high, what a sight to see,
Dad takes the first slice, oh whee!
Mom rolls her eyes, says, "Not again!"
Next to him, Aunt Sue's high on caffeine!

'Tis the season for quirky chats,
Why is the cat eyeing our hats?
Everyone laughs, the stories flow,
As we raise a toast, our cheeks all aglow!

With every bite, we share our cheer,
Gratitude's a dish we hold dear.
In quirky joy, we find our way,
These memories brighten up our day!

Echoes of Abundance

Dinner bell rings, the kids all dash,
Spilling drinks in a messy splash.
Grandpa's nap is cut quite short,
When he smells that turkey sport!

Oh, what fun and silly pranks,
Who stole the last of the sweet potato ranks?
Cousin Bill blames the family pets,
And Aunt Marge just bets, she bets!

Laughter echoes 'round the table,
As we spin tales that are quite fable.
Stuffing fights break into cheer,
This feast is one we hold so dear!

Grateful hearts and full bellies unite,
In every joke, we find delight.
Amid the chaos, we truly see,
These echoes of joy, a family spree!

Feast of Thankful Hearts

Gathering round, the table's set,
Gramps claims that last bite, you bet!
We all chuckle, it's a routine,
As he lifts that fork like a machine!

Sisters argue 'bout the best crust,
While kids make a mess—oh, that's a must!
Laughter shared, moments pure,
These funny quirks we all adore!

A pie that's gone before the count,
Who knew we had such a high amount?
Mashed potatoes, a hill too steep,
With all this joy, who needs sleep?

Thankful hearts and silly grins,
In this feast, the laughter wins.
Let's raise a glass and give a cheer,
For these funny moments, year after year!

Celebrating Everyday Wonders

In the kitchen, what a sight,
A turkey that took a flight.
Potatoes mashed with lots of glee,
Oh, where's my fork? It fled from me!

Pumpkin pie with whipped up fluff,
A slice so big, it's really tough.
A game of tug with Auntie Sue,
Who knew food could start a zoo?

Family gathers, all in cheer,
Who parked their car on Uncle's deer?
We laugh until we've lost our breath,
Then we cringe at jokes of death!

So raise a glass to all the blunders,
Life's bright moments full of wonders.
Thankful for laughter in our hearts,
Let's feast like kings—this meal's an art!

Sunlight in Moments

Sunlight dances through the leaves,
While cousin Joe attempts to weave.
A cornucopia of odd tales,
Like that one time he lost hisails.

Sisters stirring pots with flair,
One drops a spoon, it flies through air.
Grandma's smile, a beaming sun,
Sparks of joy—oh, here comes fun!

Naps are claimed like gourmet food,
Yet here we are, in merry mood.
Someone's snoring, what a treat,
While squirrels plan their great retreat.

So let us gather, tale and jest,
In every bite, we feel so blessed.
For in these moments, laughter grows,
And sunlight in our hearts bestows!

Hearts Full of Harvest

A table spread with love so wide,
Did Dad bring turkey? Nope—he tried!
To grill it in the backyard space,
Now charcoal's holding its own race.

Mom baked bread, it turned to stone,
Now we're gnawing on a bone.
Sister's dancing with the cat,
I swear that's not a real ballet spat!

Granddad spills a drink, oh dear,
Tries to wipe it, gives a cheer,
For every drop a giggle shared,
We're stuffed and laughing, all compared!

So raise a glass to every mess,
In all the chaos, we're truly blessed.
Harvest of joy, love fried and baked,
A feast so warm, hearts can't be faked!

A Melody of Grace

In the kitchen sings a tune,
While Grandma's looking like a goon.
Each pot a drum, each pan a bell,
We're the loudest band you'd ever tell.

Uncle Larry tells his jokes so sly,
Oh wait, is that a potato pie?
The oven's smoking, oh what a sight,
Like fireworks in the Sunday night!

Kids are racing, pies in hand,
Right into the dog—what a grand stand.
Now he thinks it's all for him,
Stealing bites; our chances slim.

So let's all toast to funny grace,
In every blunder, love we embrace.
From laughter's spark to snacks galore,
This melody plays forevermore!

Cherished Gatherings

In a room filled with laughter, we gather near,
A turkey that looks like it just ran a deer.
Grandma's secret recipe, we all dread,
How can one pie look like it's made of lead?

We toast to the family, so quirky and spry,
Uncles and aunts sharing tales that fly.
A nephew spills cranberry; now it's a race,
To find a new seat while we wipe our face!

Whispers of Thanks

In whispers we share, what a year it's been,
Learning dad's dance moves, it's a real win.
The cat steals a drumstick, oh what a sight,
While we all just giggle, in pure delight.

Thankful for moments, both silly and grand,
Like when cousin Billy played 'rock band.'
We sing off-key, but hey, who can blame?
We only recall laughter, not who won the game!

Bountiful Plates and Hearts

A table laden high, delights for all eyes,
But where is the pie? Oh, what a surprise!
One slice left, and it's still up for grabs,
Watch out for Auntie, she's plotting her jabs!

We dine like kings, with sweet rolls that soar,
And laughter erupts when we check the score.
Did someone just snore? Oh, Uncle Ted's done,
We'll send him the leftovers; he'll eat for fun!

Remnants of Togetherness

As plates get cleared and stories rewind,
The best of our crew are the ones we can't find.
In corners they hide, from dishes with dread,
While others recount how they once misread.

We gather the crumbs, share memories anew,
Baking up laughter, like only we do.
While leftovers linger, we treasure this time,
For it's not just the food, but the laughter that's prime!

Symphonies of the Past

Eating turkey, oh what a sight,
Gravy rivers, a true delight.
Grandpa snores, right on my plate,
I sneak a bite — can't hardly wait.

A cousin's joke, a pie in the face,
A family feud, all in good grace.
Mom's secret stuffing, we gather 'round,
A symphony of laughter, joy abounds.

Mashed potato sculpture on a chair,
A dog with leftovers, that's quite the affair.
Cheers and giggles, the night moves on,
With each silly story, we just can't be wrong.

Leftovers vanish, a miracle here,
As Uncle Bob sings a song, loud and clear.
In reflections bright, the love that we share,
In chaos and laughter, there's magic in air.

Heartfelt Homages

With each hearty bite, a thankful cheer,
We raise our glasses, someone's ear to hear.
A toast to the chef, who burnt the pie,
We laugh it off; a sweet alibi.

Granny's stories go awry again,
Last year's drama — no need to explain.
But who stole the last of the cranberry sauce?
The suspects are many, the culprit— a boss!

Sitting around, the patches of glee,
Rich tales emerge like a sweet jubilee.
Each memory seasoned, each laugh well-earned,
With every mishap, a lesson discerned.

From kitchen mayhem, our laughter grows,
As time unwinds, and the humor flows.
Together we share mischief and cheer,
Our heartfelt homages draw us near.

Roots of Abundance

Gather round, with plates oh-so-high,
Cousin Mary won't share her pie!
Roots of family run deep, they will claim,
Shared laughter and carbs, it's all just the same.

Mom's burnt rolls, a holiday gem,
Which everyone pretends to condemn.
But who needs perfection when love's on the table?
As we stuff our faces, we feel truly able.

Turkey dancing, dessert in a race,
The more we consume, the wider our space.
With leftovers waiting, fridge doors ajar,
Tomorrow's feast is not very far!

In this mix-up, we find our delight,
In the chaos of love, everything's right.
With roots of abundance, our hearts intertwine,
A feast full of laughter, together we shine.

A Gathering of Many

A gathering of many, it's quite the show,
An aunt in a hat that just can't go.
With jokes that fly like the turkey on cue,
As we chant, "Pass the stuffing!" who knew?

Cousin Tim's stories, a tad oversold,
About how he caught a fish two times as bold.
Naps ensue, as the couch starts to sway,
In the cuddly chaos, let's hope it won't stay.

Perils of sharing one tiny space,
A family that giggles, each joke leaves a trace.
Desserts piled high, we dive face-first,
The sweetest of battles, oh, we are cursed!

In dusk's gentle warmth, we wrap up the day,
With hearts full of giggles, come what may.
A gathering of many, just memories blend,
In laughter and love, we find 'tis the end.

Fragrant Reminiscence

A turkey danced across the floor,
With stuffing spilling out the door.
Grandma tried a brand new pie,
But let's not mention how it flew high.

Cousins fought for the last sweet roll,
While Uncle Fred hogged the bowl.
We giggled as the gravy poured,
And one brave soul attempted to hoard.

A toast was made to all that's grand,
While Grandpa dozed, wine glass in hand.
He snores a tune, a rhythm odd,
But we all know he's just a fraud.

With laughter echoing through the halls,
We shared the stories that time enthralls.
Though mayhem ruled the day we chose,
These fragrant memories, who wouldn't propose?

Butterflies of Blessings

Butterflies fluttered through the air,
As Auntie knit a wacky chair.
Her yarn was tangled around the cat,
He looked quite mad, we laughed at that!

Mashed potatoes, a mountain high,
But Grandma's recipe—why oh why?
With each bite, we thought we might float,
Joe claimed it tasted like a goat.

A toast was raised to everyone there,
But cups tipped over, spilled everywhere!
Uncle Joe, with a grin so wide,
Claimed he'd save a sip for pride.

In a kitchen that buzzed with cheer,
We spilled our stories, loud and clear.
With butterflies dancing in our hearts,
These blessing gatherings are true works of art!

Echoes from the Heart

Echoes of laughter greet my ear,
As Aunt Edna loudly cheers a beer.
Uncle Dave's joke was lame, but sweet,
And why he wore socks with flip-flops on his feet!

The table, laden, a sight to behold,
But the last piece of pie—oh, the stories told!
With forks held high, an epic fight,
A pie-chasing monster flashed through the night!

Grandpa's stories, in circles they fly,
Each one more ridiculous than the last, oh my!
His mustache dances as he sets the tone,
A family circus, his stage to own.

Through echoes of chatter, our hearts stay tight,
With laughter and memories, futures so bright.
Let's raise a cheer, joke, and plot,
For every goofy moment, every cherished thought!

Cherished Conversations

In cozy nooks, we gather round,
While a popcorn fight breaks without a sound.
Aunt Sue wore a turkey hat with pride,
Said it's her lucky charm for the ride!

Conversations twist and twirl like streamers,
As Dad tells tales of far-off dreamers.
With every laugh, the food grows cold,
But our spirits are warm, our stories bold!

Gravy rivers run through sincere smiles,
With jokes that stretch for endless miles.
A child's giggle pierces the air,
Did he just ask if bears can wear?

So let's toast to the quirky and kin,
To laughter, mischief, and all that's within.
In these cherished chats, we find our place,
Together we glow, a joyful embrace!

Celebrations Beneath the Autumn Sky

The turkey danced on the table,
While Auntie played her favorite fable.
Cousins fought over the last piece,
Their grumbling could never cease.

Pumpkin pies stacked way too high,
Who knew dessert could make us cry?
With laughter echoing through the halls,
No one cares about the food stalls!

The cider spilled on granddad's lap,
He laughed it off and took a nap.
Grandma's stories all rehashed,
While uncles debated who was bashed.

Oh, autumn sky, so bright and clear,
We gather round with lots of cheer.
A feast of found family and friends,
In goofy hugs, the joy never ends.

Unity in Grateful Moments

Gather round the crowded space,
With smiles and forks in every place.
Aunt Edna brought her famous stew,
And a weird dish, we didn't review.

We toast to life's quirky strife,
And how no one can cook quite right.
Laughter bubbles, stories flow,
While Uncle Joe gives his best show.

He spills red wine upon the floor,
Yells, 'I'm glad I bought one more!'
We roll our eyes, but join in glee,
For silly moments set us free.

The laughter grows, we dance and sing,
The joy and chaos that friends can bring.
Together we share our silly dreams,
In this crazy life, we find our themes.

Harvest of Gratitude

The corn maze felt like a giant joke,
Getting lost while wearing a pumpkin cloak.
We laughed till our bellies were sore,
Searching for the exit, who knew there was more?

Grandpa tried to help but got lost too,
Screaming 'This way!' only led to a boo.
But finding laughter in every turn,
Was an unexpected lesson to learn.

Moms keep reminding us to give thanks,
As we pile up mashed potatoes in big banks.
'Why not feed the turkey some pie?'
Dad rolls his eyes, we all just sigh.

As the sun sets on the fun-filled day,
We gather for hugs, and say, 'Hip-Hip-Hooray!'
For in every slice of this crazy ride,
We find love and laughter, smiling wide.

Savoring Moments in Silence

Amidst the clatter, we pause to hear,
The silence speaks, bringing us near.
But then Uncle Fred lets out a toot,
We erupt in laughter, hard to compute!

With full bellies, we bask in the calm,
Feeling thankful, the humor's the balm.
Mom's secret recipe, a total delight,
But leftovers? They'll scare us at night.

The quiet moments filled with chuckles,
As grandpa snores, he flexes his knuckles.
Reflections of love, the day's great gain,
We share in giggles, avoiding the pain.

In this tapestry of family and fun,
We cherish each other, every pun.
So let's savor silence, then raise a cheer,
For in every moment, warmth is near.

Harvesting Joy from Shared Stories

Gathered 'round the table, sharing tales,
Uncle Joe's wild antics, surely never fails.
A turkey that danced, or a pie that flew,
All giggles and snickers, just me and you.

A knock on the door, it's Aunt Betty's hat,
It's more like a bird than a fashion stat.
We can't help but chuckle, not a moment's fate,
As her stories unfold like a first date.

Cousin Tim's great plan to deep-fry a shoe,
Turned into a feast for the local zoo.
We lift our glasses, a toast to this crew,
Harvesting laughter in all that we do.

So here's to the memories, the mishaps, the fun,
With every shared moment, we've already won.
We gather our stories, as weird as they are,
In the heart of this chaos, we shine like a star.

A Time to Cherish

In a cozy old kitchen, smells waft through the air,
Mom's culinary skills, a feast beyond compare.
A pumpkin that winked, a stuffing that sings,
What joy comes together when the cooking bell rings.

The kids have gone wild, now they're chasing the cat,
Who knew this big gathering would end in a spat?
But laughter erupts as they trip on a shoe,
And all of the chaos brings smiles, it's true.

Grandpa's tall tales, of dragons and knights,
Make us question his age, are they wrong or are they right?
With each laugh we share, each cup raised up high,
We cherish these moments, they soar like a pie.

So let's pull out the photos, oh look at that dress,
When Cousin Sue danced with a pot full of mess.
It's wild and it's crazy, but what a delight,
A time to remember, our hearts feeling light.

Seasons of Thankful Memories

Leaves are falling gently, like stories from lips,
As Grandma recounts her thanks-giving trips.
When the turkey wore sunglasses, and pies played a tune,
Seasons of laughter, all bathed in the moon.

Sister's new hairstyle, a hat full of corn,
Had the neighbors all laughing from dusk until morn.
Every bite of the dinner made the table shake,
With tales of that year's epic duck-shaped cake.

Remember the time when the dog ate the pie?
We still laugh and cringe when we hear that goodbye.
Seasons are changing, but we never forget,
The moments that made us, our laughter a net.

So here's to the stories, the ones yet untold,
In the warmth of our family, both young and old.
We gather and cherish, each memory bright,
With love in our hearts, and laughter in sight.

Plates Full of Laughter

Plates full of goodies, and stories galore,
A salad that talks, yes, it's never a bore.
Grandpa just winked at a turkey that danced,
Laughter erupts, not one soul is chanced.

Dinner was served, but then came the roar,
Of Aunt Mildred's turkey, she dropped on the floor.
It bounced like a ball, oh what a sight,
Plates full of laughter drown out all the fright.

Sister's new recipe, a casserole flop,
She claimed it was magic; we covered our crop.
But amid all the giggles, we sat with delight,
Thankful for failures that made our night bright.

Let's raise our forks, give a cheer loud and clear,
To family and food, and mischief we near.
Plates full of mishaps, and laughter that brings,
In the heart of these moments, our joy always sings.

Feasts of the Heart

Turkeys tremble, pies take flight,
Grandma dances in the night.
Cranberry sauce, a wobbly sight,
Who knew leftovers could excite?

Uncles fight o'er the last slice,
Aunties gossip, oh so nice.
Kids hide sweets, a clever vice,
Our hearts are full, and so is the rice.

Laughter echoes through the hall,
Oh dear, someone dropped the ball!
Spilled gravy—now that's a call,
To join the feast, let's have a brawl!

So raise your glass, give a cheer,
To feasts and friends, all gathered here.
We'll eat our weights with no fear,
Next year's diet? Oh, disappear!

Blessings Unwrapped

Boxes piled, oh what a sight,
Taped with care, but see that fright!
Mom's new blender, what a delight,
Wait, is that a fruitcake? Yikes!

Cousins giggle, secrets shared,
What's in that box? Are we prepared?
Uncle Bob, he's always bared,
We just hope the gifts are spared.

Found some socks, a rubber duck,
Wish I knew who's out of luck.
This day brings family, oh what luck,
Just skip the gift that truly stuck!

So here's to chaos, all around,
In every present, joy is found.
Let laughter echo, it's profound,
With blessings unwrapped—a merry sound!

Echoes of Abundance

Golden crusts and buttered rolls,
Echoes of laughter, joyful souls.
Pumpkin spice and candied goals,
What's missing? Ah yes, our strolls!

Grandpa snores while we all feast,
Cousins argue over who's the least.
Tummy aches, but who's the beast?
To second helpings, we're all released!

Bellyaches have come to stay,
But who can care on such a day?
With every bite, we laugh and play,
Let's roll on out, hip-hip-hooray!

So raise a toast, take a seat,
Echoes of joy in every treat.
In this feast, we feel complete,
Abundance calls; let's hit repeat!

Light Amidst Autumn Shadows

Leaves are falling, what a sight,
Pumpkins carved with all their might.
Candles flicker, homes ignite,
What's that smell? Oh, pure delight!

Kids in costumes, giggles loud,
Running 'round, they're so proud.
Oh look, it's Grandma in the crowd,
Dancing with pie—whoa, how wowed!

Ghosts and goblins at the door,
Are we ready? Count to four!
Silly games and candy galore,
Autumn shadows, we can't ignore!

So light a fire, gather near,
With friends and family, raise a cheer.
In the chill, our hearts feel sheer,
With laughter bright, it's crystal clear!

The Colors of Appreciation

Pumpkin pie and cranberries, oh what a sight,
A feast for the eyes, and for appetite's delight.
A turkey winks at me from the big, fat line,
As gravy boats sail in a sea of divine.

My aunt's green bean casserole, a questionable hue,
We smile and we taste, while our courage is true.
With laughter and jokes, our bellies do ache,
It's the best kind of chaos, make no mistake!

Mom's wild attempts at a gluten-free roll,
End up looking like bread from a distant black hole.
We pass it around, with a giggle and cheer,
Thankful it's safe, to eat with no fear!

To all the blunders, and hats off to kin,
This colorful chaos is how we begin.
With hearts full of joy, and plates piled so high,
We toast to the moments, oh my, oh my!

Toasts to Togetherness

Raise your glass, a toast, let's make it loud,
To family and friends, oh, we're so proud!
Some burnt the stuffing, others spilled wine,
But the tales we share, make it all so fine.

Flip-flops or slippers, it's all the same,
Uncle Joe's on the couch, but he's not to blame.
He's turning redder with each passing tale,
As we roll with laughter, and graze without fail.

From toddlers to grandpas in mismatched socks,
We gather together, and who cares 'bout clocks?
With glasses held high, we cheer and we jest,
For the love that we share, truly, we're blessed!

So raise the good cheer, let the stories flow,
As we toast to this family, we all know so well.
Funny, sweet memories, they light up the day,
And that's how we gather, in our own silly way.

Candied Yams and Kind Hearts

Sweet yams on the table, they're bubbly and bright,
Mom says they're healthy; we say, 'That's alright!'
They glisten with sugar, like jewels from the earth,
Amidst all this laughing, we measure their worth.

Grandma's candied yams, the star of the night,
We dive in like pirates, it's a sugary fight.
A pinch of cinnamon, a dash of delight,
But watch for the marshmallows, they're quite a sight!

Dad's on dessert duty, but ran out of space,
He swaps his sweet potatoes for an ice cream base.
We giggle and wiggle, trying to discern,
If this was his plan - we prefer not to learn!

With hearts full of kindness, and stomachs all round,
These candied creations make laughter abound.
A feast filled with fun, let's savor each bite,
For family and food, we'll be here all night!

A Mindful Pause of Gratitude

Let's take a moment, just one or two,
To think of the messes that led us to chew.
From burnt potatoes to a pie gone awry,
It's the laughter and love that keeps spirits high.

So let's laugh about cousins who spill every drink,
And toast to sweet chaos, don't you dare overthink!
For mishaps and mix-ups are part of the play,
They flavor the feast in a unique way.

With a wink at the dog, who eyeing the spread,
We share what we love, our humor widespread.
Here's to all that's gone wrong, and all that's gone right,
We revel in comfort beneath twinkling lights.

So pause for a moment, let chuckles unfold,
With hearts full of laughter and memories bold.
We cherish these times, so silly and bright,
In gratitude's warmth, let's savor the night!

Kaleidoscope of Kindness

In a cornucopia, we stuff our glee,
Pumpkins grinning, like me and thee.
Turkey trips and stuffing fights,
Who knew we'd soar to such great heights?

Aunt Edna's pies are a sticky scene,
We laugh 'til we snort—oh, it's pretty keen!
Cousins dance with cranberry sauce,
A slip or two? Well, that's the boss!

Grateful hearts and witty jabs,
We cherish more than just the crabs.
Laughter echoes, follows the feast,
Like a wobbly chair that just won't cease!

We gather close, a big loud crew,
Life's strange flavors, like warm stew.
So let's toast to chaos and spills galore,
Thankful for laughter; who could want more?

Unity in Diversity

Gather 'round, with hats askew,
Each dish tells tales, a world view.
From tacos to turkey, what a mix,
We feast and swap our best quick tricks!

Grandpa's turkey, just a bit dry,
A family clown says, 'Hey, why not fry?'
Sisters argue, 'Last piece is mine!'
While Uncle Joe spills all the wine!

Diverse flavors, like a chef in a dream,
We blend our cultures; it's more than a theme.
Pass the stuffing to Auntie Lou,
She'll probably wear it—she's such a shoe!

Together we giggle, amidst the food fight,
This crazy gathering feels just right.
Hearts entwined despite all the fuss,
In this family, there's room for us!

Harvesting Connections

Gathered here in a patchwork quilt,
Each laugh a thread, with kindness built.
Potatoes and smiles mashed side by side,
Even the collard greens took it in stride!

Children dart like deer through the hall,
While grandma schemes for a late-night brawl.
The laughter lingers, a sweet, bright thread,
As Uncle Dan swears he'll never bake bread!

With bellies full and spirits light,
We're tangled up, and what a sight!
As we savor each quirky, yummy creation,
Building bonds in culinary elation!

We raise our glasses, with cheer all around,
In each other's hearts, our joys are found.
Harvesting warmth, that spirit so true,
In laughter and love, I'm grateful for you!

Gratitude's Gentle Embrace

In this cornfield of laughs and delights,
We juggle pies through the clumsy nights.
With each turkey leg, a story unfolds,
Of family bloopers from eons of old.

A blast of joy when the dinner bell rings,
Someone's lost their shoes, among other things.
"Pass me the gravy, not a shoe!
Can't we just eat and each say 'Boo-hoo'?"

We reminisce with an exaggerated flair,
While cousin Gary dons grandma's hair.
Together we cheer, the good and the bad,
For these silly moments, we're all just glad!

A chorus of chuckles fill the air,
With each blunder, a wild love affair.
So here's to the mess, the smiles we share,
In laughter, we grow, a family rare!

Abundant Harvests

Pumpkins stacked, a funny sight,
Cranberry sauce, oh what a fright!
Stuffing fights, a culinary brawl,
Mashed potatoes ready to take a fall.

Turkey dancing on the plate,
Family debates on who's quite late.
Pies that wobbly wiggle and charm,
Keep your forks away from the farm!

Gravy rivers flow like a stream,
Uncle Joe's snoring, what a dream!
Sweet potato smiles and corn on the cob,
All share a plate, all share a job.

Laughter bursts with each silly toast,
Mom's burnt pie? We love it the most!
An abundant feast with quirks and delight,
Let's eat until the stars shine bright.

Moments Woven with Care

A table set, but who spilled the beans?
The dog, not me, that's how it seems.
Glances dart like squirrels in a tree,
Who took the last roll? Not guilty, you see!

Napkin hats worn with much pride,
Grandpa's jokes—did they take a ride?
Cousin Alice with pie on her nose,
We all laugh as the craziness grows.

Leftover turkey? Let's have some fun,
Craft sandwiches that weigh a ton!
Mom says "eat your broccoli," oh dear,
Hide it well, or share with a deer.

These moments stitched with giggles and yum,
Thankful for tadpoles and popcorn gum.
Reflections of laughter, stories to share,
In our hearts, forever laid bare.

Heartstrings and Honey

Honey drips from the biscuits we bake,
Sweetness in laughter, and love's give-and-take.
Auntie's hugs wrap us warm, oh so tight,
As we juggle the butter in culinary flight.

Heartstrings tug, when Grandma appears,
Her stories adorned with giggles and cheers.
Potato peels flying, what a surprise!
We'll clean it all up—well, that's the prize!

"Don't forget the pie!" shouts a small voice,
We sing and we dance, oh what a choice!
Pumpkin spice lingers, warm and divine,
Let's dance 'til the stars align!

With honeyed laughter, we savor the day,
Creating memories in our zany array.
Heartstrings and sweetness, a comical stare,
Together we flourish, sweet moments to share.

The Table of Togetherness

Gather 'round with faces aglow,
Who knew broccoli could cause such a show?
Tablecloths shimmering, set with great flair,
But Auntie Ham's stories? We barely can bear!

With every forkful, we giggle and tease,
"Stop stealing my turkey!" with accusations that tease.
Silly hats made from napkins and fun,
When food meets laughter, it's all just begun!

Friends and family, a delightful clash,
Food fights may erupt with a splash!
Mashed potato sculptures, high as the wall,
"Bravo!" we cheer, as they start to fall.

Together we munch, together we cheer,
Each bite wrapped in joy, sprinkled with cheer.
A table adorned with laughter's embrace,
In this chaos of joy, we find our place.

A Festival of Reflections

Gather 'round the turkey, it's all a big tease,
Who knew that bird would give us such ease?
Uncle Tim's jokes are older than dirt,
But we laugh till it hurts, in joy and in mirth.

Cousin Sue stirs the pot, a curious brew,
With mashed potatoes that look like glue.
A splash of gravy, a dash of a smile,
And the chaos of kids makes it all worthwhile.

Grandma's pie serves more than just taste,
It's a weapon of choice, there's no time to waste.
"Who ate my leftovers?" she cries with a frown,
But we're all in the clear, we just pass around.

In this feast of delights, it's clear what we find,
Laughter and friends, the best of mankind.
So raise up your glass with no time to spare,
For the moments we share, beyond all compare.

Seeds of Appreciation

A giant feast on our old picnic table,
With dishes piled high, but are we really able?
Stuffing so rich, you question your plans,
One more slice? Oh, who's got the hands?

Auntie's sweet potatoes, they glow like the sun,
While Uncle Bob claims he's just here for fun.
His dance moves are wild, his rhythm an art,
We're all cracking up, right from the start.

Gratitude flows with each clink and each cheer,
While Dad tries a dad joke, we all disappear.
"Why did the turkey cross the road?" he will jest,
We just shove in more pie, let the humor digest!

So here's to the harvest, hilarious and pure,
With laughter to sow, our hearts shall endure.
Come gather around, bring all your delight,
For this banquet of silliness, oh what a sight!

Warmth in Gathered Souls

As family arrives, the door's thrown wide,
A whirlwind of hugs and uncontrolled pride.
Pet socks on the table—oh, look at that mess,
But who needs perfection? It's all just a guess!

Grandpa insists we all try his stew,
"Just trust me, it's wonderful, it's something new!"
With noodles like snakes and a splash of the red,
We all share a taste, then run off instead.

The laughter erupts when the pie takes a tumble,
A splat on the floor, oh, what a big fumble!
But we find all the humor in every small blunder,
As we snack through the night, laughing loud like thunder.

So here's to the warmth, to wit and to glee,
In the foolishness shared, it's just you and me.
With hearts full of laughter and bellies so tight,
We celebrate together, what a sheer delight!

Savory Skies of Thanks

Plates piled high with a colorful spread,
And Aunt Linda's casserole, a legend, it's said.
A bite from her dish, a mystery unfolds,
Like a magical quest where the flavor beholds!

Kids dart around, with plates that are stacked,
While trying to hide from Aunt Betty's whacked.
"Eat more of this!" she yells as we flee,
It's amusingly tragic—oh, let us be free!

The dog's taste-testing while we watch and we cheer,
As he snags a roll—oh dear, have no fear!
Grandma just giggles, the scene is surreal,
With moments like these, it's a wonderful meal.

With a toast to the madness, the fun that we share,
We capture these moments, like fresh autumn air.
In this festive affair, with laughter galore,
All these savory skies leave us yearning for more!

Threads of Generosity

Around the table, we gather, we feast,
Grandma's special dish—oh, not quite a beast!
Uncle Joe nearly drops, that big turkey weight,
Laughter erupts, as he joins the plate fate.

With each golden roll, we share our delight,
Who stole the last piece? It was quite a sight!
A pie flies through air, as cousin sneezes,
We all duck in time, oh, life's little breezes.

My aunt's secret sauce, it's something to try,
But who knew it glows? Like a disco, oh my!
We munch and we giggle, despite all the dread,
Last year's fruitcake still lingers in dread.

So raise up your glasses, let's toast and let flow,
To all of our blessings, and odd little shows!
With each joyful bite, our spirits will cheer,
In this quirky moment, we hold ever dear.

The Spice of Togetherness

Pass the potatoes, oh what a delight,
But wait, it's a food fight, who threw that tonight?
A grand uncle's grin, like a kid in a store,
'Can we borrow your hat? We're all wanting more!'

A sprinkle of laughter, a dash of a smile,
A pinch of confusion, oh it's worth the while!
Cookies that crumble are evidence near,
A three-second rule, when desserts disappear.

The gravy boat tips, oh what a mishap,
We leap without grace, try to avoid the flap.
The dog joins the fray, he's stealing the treats,
While Grandma just winks, and nods her head beats.

So gather around, it's a bumpy old ride,
With mischief and joy, we take it in stride!
Each bite, each slip, is a blessing to share,
In our own little chaos, we find love's true flair.

Quilts of Kindness

Under quilted laughter, we snugly abide,
Recipes tangled, like yarn intertwined.
Cousins start whispering, 'Did you hear that joke?'
Uncle's naps disrupted? Oh, what a bloke!

Each slice of the cake, it's a world gone wild,
A little too moist? Call it Grandma's child!
A pie chart of bites, how did we stray?
But who's keeping score? It's just fun, hooray!

The tales shared around, they twist and they loop,
While granddad's gone fishing with half of the group.
It's all a bit messy, but love spills and glows,
Binding us closer, with each laugh that flows.

So let's knit together, with threads from the past,
A tapestry woven, with smiles that last.
With forks and our hearts, we'll cherish this time,
In life's playful quilt, we find our sweet rhyme.

Lifting Hearts in Harmony

With jingle of laughter, we start the parade,
A dance in the kitchen, hope none are delayed!
Bubbling pots sing, like a quirky old tune,
While Aunt Sally twirls like a big blooming balloon.

The cider flows freely, we toast to the mess,
A clumsy tradition we all just profess.
Someone slips on the floor, oh what a scene!
Who knew that the cat would be such a queen?

We pile on the couch, like a heap of delight,
A game of charades, oh, what a weird sight!
The laughter erupts as we figure it out,
With goofy responses that poke and that pout.

So here's to the squabbles, the hugs and the cheer,
For every odd moment we hold ever dear.
Together we flourish, with spirits we sway,
In this bonkers delight, let's shout hip-hip-hooray!

Echoes of Gratitude

Turkeys playing hide and seek,
Where did they go? Oh, it's quite bleak!
Pumpkin pie sings a sweet refrain,
In the fridge, it dances with disdain.

Family feuds over who to blame,
For burnt rolls that look quite the same.
Gravy spills like a fountain of fun,
As laughter echoes; we've all just begun.

Sitting around like peas in a pod,
Uncle Joe's tales—sometimes a facade.
We nod and smile, suppressing a snort,
Who knew the feast would be such a sport?

With every bite, an awkward look shared,
Counting blessings—we're all a bit scared.
Yet amidst all the chaos and cheer,
We stick together, year after year.

A Mosaic of Togetherness

Gathered 'round like mismatched socks,
Grandma's famous casserole rocks!
A dance in the kitchen, a twist and a spin,
Bob's mysterious dish—what's hiding within?

Kids run wild with cranberry stains,
Dogs and cats vie for crusty remains.
The table's wobbling, laughter spills,
With every toast, the silliness thrills.

Granny's stories take silly flights,
As we blame the dog for our food fights.
Leftovers hide like treasures untold,
Each bite holds memories, funny and bold.

At day's end, tired hugs all around,
Contentment and giggles in each sound.
Though we're messy and somehow askew,
In this zany mosaic, we're stuck like glue.

Cauldron of Connection

In a bubbling pot of laughter and glee,
A dash of chaos, a sprinkle of tea.
Will Aunt Patty ever get the recipe right?
Or will we feast on her famous fright?

Dancing spoons and a soup on the floor,
Try not to laugh, oh, what a chore!
The roast clatters like a cymbal's tune,
As Cousin Tim trips under the moon.

Gravy rivers flow down our plates,
While we debate who ate the last baked?
Chitters and chatters spark up the night,
With each silly tale, our spirits take flight.

A mix of flavors, humorous and wild,
Bonds are formed, like that of a child.
In this cauldron where memories blend,
Laughter and love, a recipe to defend!

A Canvas of Kindness

Brush strokes of laughter paint the air,
With every mishap, we show we care.
Mistakes in the kitchen? They're just art!
Each burnt pie is a masterful part!

Family portraits of silly and bold,
Gravy mustaches that never grow old.
As we wipe the table, we spill a few tales,
Of triumphs, flops, and festive fails.

With every meal, we gather 'round tight,
To share in the joy and embrace the light.
The satisfaction in laughter we find,
On this colorful canvas, all hearts are combined.

So here's to the moments we can't recreate,
To every sticky finger and wild plate.
In this joyous jumble, we make our stand,
Grateful together, hand in hand.

Milton Keynes UK
Ingram Content Group UK Ltd.
UKHW021938121124
451129UK00007B/136